THE WAGES OF LOVE

William Meredith Poetry Award Citation

Christie Max Williams is a well-known Connecticut actor, poet, and impresario. The exquisite poems in his first collection (published by Antrim House,) recount his love of women, children, and fatherhood. A lifetime as a footsoldier in the arts has prepared him for the mastery of language and the charming appreciation of the "good bind" he finds himself in at the joyful human moment demonstrated in his poems. They fulfill the highest potential of poetry: to teach, yes, but importantly, to delight. To paraphrase Saint Paul, the wages of love is life.

Richard Harteis, President of the William Meredith Foundation

THE WAGES OF LOVE

Poems by

Christie Max Williams

Antrim House
Bloomfield, Connecticut

Library of Congress Control Number: 2022903422

ISBN: 978-1-943826-98-8

First Edition, 2022

Printed & bound by Ingram Content Group

Book design by Rennie McQuilkin

Author photograph by A. Vincent Scarano

Cover painting by Kathleen Kucka

Antrim House
860.519.1804
AntrimHouseBooks@gmail.com
www.AntrimHouseBooks.com
400 Seabury Dr., #5196, Bloomfield, CT 06002

To Catharine

and to Tess and Cody

ACKNOWLEDGMENTS

Many thanks to the editors of the following publications in which these poems first appeared:

Grace, 'Step One' and 'Kingdom'
Grolier Annual, 'His Hands' and 'Hard Night'
Post, 'Bistro du Nord'
Sonnet, 'Bethlehem, Again' and 'House'
The Day, 'Needing a Bath'
The Mystic Times, 'On Occasion'

I'm deeply glad for this opportunity to thank the early readers of this work: Margaret Gibson, Gray Jacobik, Stephen Dobyns, Lisa Starr, Richard Harteis, and Paul Barber. Their encouragement and criticism have helped, I hope, to make me a better poet and make *The Wages of Love* a better book. It seems to me that no debut poet can ever have been better served than I by these supportive and talented friends.

Thanks also to my friends and poets of the Savoy poetry group who have listened to many of these poems. I'll buy the next round!

Special thanks are reserved for my editor, publisher, and friend, Rennie McQuilkin, for his immense patience, insistent good taste, and dependable kindness.

Heartfelt thanks are also due the William Meredith Foundation for plucking *The Wages of Love* out of obscurity by conferring on it the William Meredith Poetry Award – a cherished prize in the name of a cherished poet.

Lastly, to my much-loved first reader, dearest friend and spouse, Catharine Moffett – gratitude for your love and support is the subtext to every poem I write.

TABLE OF CONTENTS

III. BISTRO DU NORD

That love is all there is,
Is all we know of love;
It is enough, the freight should be
Proportioned to the groove.

Emily Dickinson

We must love one another or die.

W.H. Auden

THE WAGES OF LOVE

The Wages of Love in 2020

Afterward
we sprawled, a fleshy heap,
molten, warm,
sticky here and there,
aroma thick and feral.
Arms were gone askew,
legs entangled,
hands irrelevant.
Amid the mess of bedding
skin felt timeless,
cheek pressed to shoulder,
belly to butt,
lips undone, turned blousy,
time itself undone,
time itself irrelevant.
Well-being had become both mindless and mindful,
we, all but immortal –
gone the government's venality,
gone its daily lies –
we, a congress of contentment,
we, the president of pleasure,
at once full and void,
an end, a new beginning:
the wages of love is life.

I. LOVE AND DEATH

The wages of sin is death; but the gift of God is eternal life.
Romans 6, 23

The only secret people keep is immortality.
Emily Dickinson

The wages of dying is love.
Galway Kinnell

The Beauty of Drowning in Southern California

They were a glory din of bigger boys
and *I* – I was a dark uncertainty,
a small shy scheme of a boy hunched
by the edge of the magnolia-shaded shallows
of that backyard swimming pool,
in whose boisterous water
my dangling feet were stirring secret plans.

Then all at once the other boys,
like autumn geese exploding into flight,
burst large and laughing from the pool,
their slashing rapid bodies flocking raucously indoors,
for they were a party commanded by someone's mother,
while I was a little brother quietly invisible
where I'd been left beside the pool:
and it was what I *wanted*.

The calm was sudden
in the jasmine-scented backyard garden,
sudden, too, the water's silence at the pool's far end,
its silky ice-blue surface undulant beneath the sun's hypnotic pulse,
the light's intensity a dazzling invitation,
and yet from having watched the plunges of the bigger boys
I knew the water there was deep:
but it was *also* what I wanted,
to swim like them,
like them to delve into the water's silence.

Soundlessly I slid into the pool,
slithered snake-like down into the cool-warm silky water,
for, like the snake, I was determined
to be neither missed nor noticed,
and though my feet touched bottom still,

my hands held hard on to the beveled edge
that lipped around the pool,
held hard on to my secret plan
as hand by hand I slowly edged my way
toward deeper water.

It was at the pool's far end I stopped,
stopped where I sensed the water to be deepest,
and there the world waited,
the jasmine-scented silent light
of that particular California *waited*,
waited as my small shy scheme clung to the edge –
and it was there that I let go.

What happened next I hadn't planned for –
as, expecting that my body like the goosey bigger boys'
would take to wing upon the water,
I was instead surprised
to feel my face slip easily beneath the surface,
surprised my eyes could clearly see within the water world,
as drifting downward,
easing smoothly through the slow dense calm of that aquatic ether,
I felt no fear,
felt fortunate luxuriating in its liquid light,
bedazzled by the patterned squares surrounding me,
square by inscrutable blue square
a mystery repeated for my meditative drift,
before, beside, behind me,
a radiant redundancy of geometric turquoise blue –
until with an ecstatic suddenness
I recognized them as ceramic tiles,
the turquoise tiles that squarely walled the pool!
and in the moment's recognition
I conceived of them as *beautiful* –
until with drowsy ease
I touched the darkness at the bottom of the pool.

And *beautiful* it was,
the turquoise tile radiance
whose color I would recognize again
in older ecstasies on Costa Rican shores –
beautiful the very word
my boy's particular of mind invoked to name that blue,
a word I had not known I knew,
as beauty was a vision I had yet to see, though knew on sight –
and O how *beautiful* my brother
who found me, still and curled,
asleep upon the pool's maternal lap,
and by whose saving breath I live to tell.

First Blood

Then I heard it,
the long slow screech of skidding tires on pavement.

In church,
a small strange boy in thrall to finger fidgets
I raised my head and listened
to the prolonged road shriek,
listened as it ceased with a concussive crash
of steel and glass – then sudden stillness.

Was it sound or silence that
reverberated in my restless mind?
And why had no one else looked up?
Had they heard it? Had I?

After prayers,
after what seemed distant sirens,
after punch and cookies on the sunny patio among
the grown ups with their cigarettes and coffee,
I asked my folks if I might walk
the few streets home from church –
then unobserved I headed to my secret path,
the beaten track of dirt between
the forest of oleanders by the road
where I was certain no one else would be.

The skinny trail was baked and hard,
the canopy of oleanders shifted with the breeze,
and then as always on that path I felt
that something was about to happen.

And suddenly there was a shiny shard of steel
which wasn't there a week ago,

curved, fist-sized, a hole at one end.
I held and fingered it until, just ahead,
a glint of glass distracted me,
smaller than a marble, a jagged nugget
tinged a pale clear aquamarine,
and kneeling to it, holding it,
I peered through a gash in the oleanders to the road
where on the pavement a splash
of glassy nuggets glistened in the sun.

Then I was stopped –
stopped where I had almost stepped –
the tips of Sunday shoes a step from it –
a shining puddle in the path,
a puddle brilliant red,
a redness new to me.

The world was still
as squatting on my haunches I considered it,
reached and touched a finger to the puddle's surface,
drew the red-tipped finger up,
thought to taste it,
realized it must be blood.

I wondered if it could be God I felt,
but decided it was not.
And yet what was that light?
What was that sound, that smell, that taste –
what else but death's pure aura?
In that bright stillness a shudder worked my spine –
then I, myself, grew still and understood –
I too would someday die.

The day was bright and warm,
life was deeply strange and new,
but I was not afraid –
I did not understand to be afraid.

House

A little house of greying shingles, say,
with bright red shutters and a warped red door
opening on a crooked porch which may
or may not creak when the wind's onshore;
an old sea-humbled cottage, if you will,
leeward leaning, indifferently snug,
the salt-swell warping every window sill,
the sand recalcitrant in every rug –
a gangly bungalow with peeling paint
and closet doors which will not shut when told,
a place of memories near or faint,
a beach for holding hands and growing old.
In time its hearth will grow as cold as dirt
upon a grave. Yes, a life may sweetly hurt.

Grackle

Look, a sudden grackle on the green –
there, that pulsing blue-black iridescence –
see how it cocks its golden eye, keen
to stab its beak into some wiggling essence.
Among the worms, the grackle is a god,
the great *I am,* gorging in the grass,
unfixed, unfathomed, fiercely unflawed,
and lo, since miracles may come to pass,
behold the grackle bursting into flight,
its fanning wings like twin black flames
ignited by a grim divine delight,
vanishing in glories without names.
A god, it seems, may come and go.
The chance of love is all that's left to us below.

Prayer in Berkeley

Rain. Late at night.
Tired, I left the warm library
walking into town on Telegraph,
the street and sidewalks empty,
the slow steady rattle of rain on pavement
was all there was –
the rain had fallen ceaselessly for days.
Though in my hooded poncho I was almost dry,
below the knees my jeans were sodden,
my leather boots beleaguered, squishy –
the world was cold, wet, and dark.

Veering off the avenue,
headed to my rented room,
I nearly passed the iron staircase
slanting to a basement door –
but sitting on the stairs,
hunched over, head bowed, yet sheltered from the rain,
a young woman.

I stopped, peered at her, said
'Are you all right?'

She looked up at me with shining eyes,
not startled, but slow
as though awakened.

'Are you all right?'
I asked more gently.

'I was praying,' she replied.

She was very young, my age perhaps,
perhaps like me a student.
Her hair was long and wild;
she seemed feral, yet gentle, fragile.

'I was only praying,' she said.

It was probably the angle of the streetlight
but her face glowed,
giving off a sort of aura –
she was lovely.

'I'm all right,' she said
kindly as if to care for *me* –
kindly seeming to observe
that I was standing in the rain.

I gazed at her eyes,
disconcerting, large and luminous –
until the moment became awkward.

Okay, I might have said.
Take care, perhaps.

What did I want?
Was it her?
Her god?
I wanted something –
I may want it still.

I remember I walked home, cold and hungry.

Goethe in California

O to be young in California,
to be blessed and cursed with a mind on fire!

There we gathered,
the hopeful best and brightest of our generation,
gathered outside that hallowed hall of learning
in the mid-day sunshine of a swelling spring,
circled on the new-mowed lawn
beneath that blooming cherry tree.

She too arrived, aglow,
amazed all too apparently by life,
though smiling shyly if slyly at me,
for lately I had taught her how to kiss,
a willing pupil
though apt to let her teeth click eagerly on mine.

'I'm reading something so far out,' she said –
'it's called *The Stranger* –
by a French guy - AL-burt KAM-muss.'

'Al-BARE Cam-MOO,' I interrupted
in my freshly honed though fledgling French,
'and it's *L'Etranger*,' I finished with a flourish,
scarcely noticing her flashing eyes,
her flushed cheeks,
her mute humiliation,
as I proceeded to hold forth on Camus' *Sisyphus*,
on human toil and suffering in a godless world,
on man's responsibility to make a meaning of compassion.

But the book I was combustible about
was Geth-ee's *Sorrows of Young Wur-ther*,

its Sturm and Drang,
its tragic beauty of an unrequited love –and how I soared,
like a German eagle in my wild flight –
until another of our gathering, a friend,
spoke up to say 'I think you may mean GUR-tuh'. . .

The world stopped.
'What?' I gasped
and felt all eyes fixed on my face.

The air was still.
The sun was in my eyes.
I could not breathe.

'And it's Ver-ter, not Wur-ther,' he added with a helpful smile.

Goethe Goethe Goethe!
What sinister and senseless sort of world
would say or spell a great man's name that way?

I may have nodded in reply but surely didn't speak.
In my humiliation, utterly unutterable,
I looked to her,
and meeting with her eyes I was amazed
to see in them the very color of compassion.

Nocturne

1.

You, peering deep into the night,
having wakened weak with grief
to hours of unrelenting insight –

you, abandoned by belief,
in that too familiar room, alone,
yearning for sleep's unreal relief –

know that your solitary groan
is heard: know that your darkened care
cuts close to the common bone –

within the mind of that spindly chair
or deep inside the bed's uncertain frame,
even in the window's bare black stare

your pain is greeted as if by name.
Imagine that the tender pardon
you have sought requires no shame –

conceive of silence as a garden
where the thinking heart may green
a meaning. Trust that *your* heart will not harden –

because if fading gods don't intervene,
nothing means but what *you* mean.

2.

So, the night has summoned you once more,
and like a man condemned you mark the hours
'til dawn cracks open the day's grim door.

What's left of hope the time devours,
and yet you fear the night may never end:
darkness sprouts such anxious flowers.

But nothing is ever as you intend –
wind blows, a sparrow shifts its perch,
the moon continues to ascend:

still, in what way does the autumn birch
intend to lose its last gold leaf?
There is no purpose in the search –

there is only the brave motif
of being: *be* the meaning of the night;
be the object of your own belief.

Truly you have been given the night
to know: know it as your deeper part:
close the book; switch off the light –

listen: it's the beating of your heart,
the steady beating of your heart.

3.

Yes, the night is vast and you are not –
its tide of darkness floods your mind,
engulfing action, drowning thought

as there you drift, inert, too blind
to wonder – and yet, what is that smell?
that apprehension un- or ill-defined

which even sleep will not dispel?
that cold faint foulness always there,
seeping as from a deep but tainted well?

Is it failure's scented snare,
the chill of decomposing dreams,
or is it the perfume of fresh despair?

If you seek its source, it seems
so near – *too* near. But can you *be*
and fail to be what life redeems?

Though drifting on the night's vast sea,
though north and south have fallen off your chart,
the compass points at you unfailingly.

You are the destination. Start
to swim: a guiding current will give you heart.

Autumn Night

Our room is ocean-dark.
Outside, the woods obscure the glinting stars,
but in the heavy night I catch
the spicy fragrance of the early autumn Earth
and hear my lover's mighty draw and heave of breath.
Urgently she sucks the dark air in
and pauses – as if to savor it –
then the long slow exhalation,
pivot point and engine shift,
concluding with a vast more dreadful halt,
a deep and empty silence, like
the airless hush before a hurricane –
no, like death, like the moment's realization
that there will be no further moments.
Involuntarily my hand embarks
across the sea of darkness, landing
on the flank shore of her naked knee –
hard bone, taut tendon, cool soft skin –
and at my sudden touch she starts
to breathe again, but different now –
calm, silent, a shallow panting, conveying
aboriginal alertness, poised anticipation, waiting –
it is the animal connection – life magic.
The rest is sleep.

Ninth Avenue Food Festival

Then I saw her.

Early, perched there on the curb a
spying distance from our meeting place,
like some discordant Cold War stake out,
I watched for her.
Wanting to observe her prior to proceeding,
wanting to be less uncertain,
I watched.
Weeks had passed since we'd been introduced
and I had yet to see her in the light of day –
then she was there.

At 23rd and Ninth,
in the bulls eye of that crossroads cordoned for the festival –
the gustatory festival that was our destination –
which if things did not work out
could gracefully be terminated,
even while the night still glamorously loomed –
but then I saw her.

In the noontime brilliance of that early June
she stood expectant, searching – straight and shining –
hair sharply bobbed, hip shades – an edgy almost beauty.
I was there because we'd talked well on the phone.
I was there because I hungered for fresh light –
but lately liberated from the prison of a sad spent marriage,
I had no appetite to plot another nuptial crime:
I had already done the world too much selfish harm.

Yet, standing there among the multitude –
like Jesus just before he sat upon
the ass that bore him to Jerusalem –
I felt a something that I could not name,

sensed it might be destiny,
was momentarily amused, appalled by this absurdity,
then mustering a sweet determination
I cleaved into the merry crowd in her direction,
saw she might be pretty,
saw her turn and smile to see me,
and all the world was a festival.

She was vivacious, an occasion,
as we strolled up Ninth,
past the gaily colored stalls,
through sweetly cloying clouds of frying pastry dough,
through aromatic wafts of grilling meats.
But we weren't hungry yet –
there was so much to say.
I said there was a showing at the Modern
of Truffaut's film *Jules and Jim*,
at 2, 4, 6, and 8 o'clock –
she too had never seen it,
she too had always wanted to,
she said so with a smile that was beguilingly intelligent.

But at 2
the day was far too fine to plunge into a movie house.
Instead we drank a beer from plastic cups,
shared sausages and peppers from a paper plate,
and talked.

At 4, or just before,
still mindful of both 6 and 8 o'clock,
we crossed into the park,
slurped party-colored popsicles,
and talked some more.
Yes, destiny can be like that.

Sometime just before or after 6
we sat upon the rocky ledge above the boat pond
and having for the moment nothing else to say,
we kissed.

At 8
she opened an enlightening Pomerol
in her apartment.
We sat and talked about the day
and luckily the movie didn't show at 10:
love is sometimes just like that.

At home, at last, the evening after,
like Prometheus in chains,
I asked myself *What have I done?*
even while savoring the taste of destiny.
It was a few years after that
we finally caught *Jules et Jim*,
which, after talking, we agreed was terrible.

Naked

for Catharine

Naked, moonlike in the dusk, you rise
above my frozen field full and white,
your slow insightful feet and flashing thighs
dancing – dancing their curved and urgent light.

Naked you wait, like a rock in rain,
ecstatically enduring Spring's rough measure,
each drop upon your skin a shining stain
of deep impassioned pleasure.

Naked you lie speckled in the sun,
like a too ripe peach dropped from a high limb,
split open, juices leaking, flesh undone,
your fertile pit imagining its fragrant climb.

Naked like smoke you curl articulate
above my smoldering fire,
your ghostly voice intoning delicate
demands into the darkened corners of desire.

Naked your eyes of sea and sky,
naked your open hand, like a nest, a haven.

Naked your hair of wheat,
naked your belly, like a morning in July, the warmth
    before the heat.

Naked your heart, like a bird singing,
like a warbler in the instant before springing into flight,

naked.

Uptown Bus

It was already late.
But really, isn't it always late?

When at last the bus arrived
I found my place in back,
holding the pole for lack of seats,
idling my thoughts for want of inspiration,
when a sudden voice called out my name,
and turning, 'Sue,' I said to the flash
of her inquiring smile, surprised
her name had sprung so readily to mind.

Seeing her, I thought of *you*,
beloved, my new and current, my only you.

She stood and joined me at the pole,
grasping with a gloved hand,
a loosely knit cashmere grey glove
strange and beautiful on that fine September day,
even as I gazed perhaps intently at her face
like a man long gone from home
who after hardship beholds again his native land.

This is another life that still could be.
This is another kind of *we*.

She was pretty still,
pretty her smooth olive skin,
her clear brown eyes, and aureole of black curls,
and with that smile she asked me how I was –
indeed, how was I?
and shouldn't I have said I was in love?
'Fine,' I said though it has never been the case,
'I'm fine too,' she said without me asking,

then kindly asked 'Have you been getting work?'
a question that I hadn't heard in years.

> I might have said of *you,*
> *You're all the work that I can do.*

Years before, Sue'd played Ismene
to my Oedipus, both Rex and At Colonus
in repertory weeks off-Broadway,
costumed and painted like Greek vases
by a mad and all-too-Greek director
whose vision of the drama's tragic agon
saw the female chorus bare and beat their lovely breasts,
even as the hapless hero became all too naked
at the sight of poor Jocasta hanging –
a kind of work if you can get it.

> Had I become another kind of man?
> It *seemed* I was another kind of man.

I hadn't seen this Sue since the morning after
that final fateful night of Oedipus,
but it was Ismene and her father/brother
who became naked that night in Sue's apartment,
a twist of comic fate at least as sweet
as Sophocles might have imagined –
her body glowing in soft light
through that long and fragrant interlude . . .
In the morning I went home
to a betrayed and bitter spouse.

> Untethered, uncommitted, improvised,
> Then as ever, at my life too much surprised.

'I'm married now,' said Sue 'and pregnant too,'
smiling, looking frank and straight into my eyes.

'I'm a hand model,' she added.
'It's why I wear these gloves – see,' she said,
removing one, showing me a smooth and glowing hand.
'Wonderful,' I think I said sincerely,
her eyes still holding mine,
but then it was her stop, the bus door opened,
and in the usual way we smiled,
shook hands, and wished each other well,
as wondering I clung still to the pole,
as streets and minutes must have passed.

O shouldn't I have said I was in love with you?
Which was and still is true.

Immortality

(while awaiting the subway)

What did she see,
that young and purely solitary woman
standing in the cool gray silence of the subway stop

as though composed by a photographer,
book in hand, intently reading,
her coral lips and quilted sky-blue coat

the only colors in that timeless light –
what did she see, as looking up
amid the turning of a page, her eyes met mine?

Perhaps I was a man
no longer of an age to hope
for her reciprocal regard,

though the truth is it was not at her
that I'd been looking,
or should I say not *only* at her,

but at the book
in which she was so deeply steeped
I had to know its title.

My eyes were good
though not as good as they used to be –
what is?

So as if to scan the twilit track
for the train I hoped would be delayed,
I took an oblique step not quite towards her,

until just glimpsing the elusive cover
of her book, just as her languid hand
turned over that transforming page,

just as her breasts rose up then subtly set
on the impassioned breath she drew,
which seemed in turn to lift her chin,

the dying cadence in a melody of motion
I could not help but follow –
until her eyes met mine.

What did *I* see
if not a shining instant of her wonder –
if not the lingering light reflected from

whatever fire burned within the words just read?
which in the moment of my marveling
was suddenly eclipsed

by her perception of whatever darkness skulked
in my beholding mind –
was smothered by a gathering gloom

of fear, contempt, and violation –
for *something had been violated* –
and in the mute unmeaning moment

of that cool gray gulf of time and space
she turned her back to me,
retreated up the platform,

then deftly re-composed herself,
her sky-blue back still turned,
the open book once more in hand.

The very silence tittered at my shame even as a
plaintive voice within me cried
No please! You don't understand!

I'm not like other men – I, too, read books –
For me as well as you
a fateful train will all too soon arrive . . .

I might have crossed to where she stood
and might have said these things,
but history cast its iron shadow

even on my dumb paralysis,
since in New York it's dangerous
for strangers at a subway stop

to seek an understanding.
And yet, how can I *not* remember
that her eyes were blue

and that the title of her book was *Immortality*?

Stars for Susan

Where are you, friend? I need your voice, your face.
I long to watch you listening to me,
to know myself a glowing commonplace
in your affection, to feel you simply be.
O meet me at the usual café,
yes, the one where I am always late,
where the wine makes no demands on what we say,
where we can be a night to celebrate.
At the same quiet table sit the ghosts
of our best selves, waiting to be moved
to laughter – or is it tears? For them let's toast
the luck and mystery of being loved.
Later, passing shuttered shops and bars,
suppose we stop, look up – there might be stars!

Long Walk with a Good Friend

For Alan

Two, men, we stood in the autumn light
of your apartment, like caged and aging lions
who haven't yet forgot the beauty of the hunt,

and after a respectful pause you replied,
'it's always seemed to me
that if you want to *be* a good man,

behave like one,
behave as you conceive a good man would,
and your behavior will become your being.'

What could I say to this?
You held my gaze that moment like an open question,
then with a sudden shrug you chuckled

at having made so nearly pompous a pronouncement,
and I, too, shrugged and cleared my throat,
as one man should at another man's embarrassment,

but I was troubled with the truth of it –
there was humility and darkness in your eyes,
there were failings and regret,

and perhaps the deep shadow of shame –
you had known some life – your mirth was earned.
You were a man, though somehow unlike other men.

*   *   *

Then we walked out to the street,
to an afternoon of golden light,
and decided we were headed to the river,

even as the city met us like a smiling host,
gracious, glad to see us,
though rushed with many other guests to greet.

The streets felt festive, filled with people
cast in countless conversations,
busy with good will and places still to go,

and the café tables beckoned as we passed,
the street-fair stalls reached out
seductively with tired and funny colors,

but we were bound and headed to the river,
even as I struggled to keep pace with you,
your stride as always long and loping,

and while we walked, we talked –
of your fresh sorrows, which we touched on tenderly,
and of your pain, which you were sure was nothing to speak of,

and so we spoke of women, of places we had seen –
and though it may have been impossible to say
just what we meant, we said it anyway and no one noticed.

*   *   *

We knew the streets along the way,
but as so often happens they had changed
from what we'd known so well,

but still, we *believed* in the walk –
it was our sacrament, the city our cathedral –
we believed in that day with a simple faith,

yet when at last we came upon the river,
the sun was near to setting,
while up and down the esplanade the people passed,

so many and so many kinds of people on parade,
it seemed a sort of celebration,
it seemed somehow they were saluting our arrival.

The sun was burnishing a path across the river,
and the spectacle of sunset and parade
seemed to be happening *for you,*

to be a tribute to your happiness in being there,
and I was moved to say so – but didn't –
certain that a good man never would.

French Kiss

When I burned bright, Paris alone was true
and life was art (or was it the other way around?)
– Paris is where I am when I'm with you.

Through endless café nights in drizzly rue
Saint Jacques, my genius fevered to be found –
when I burned pure, Paris was truly true.

Bravely I stormed those barricaded blue-
white-and-red French hearts – bohemian unbound!
– Paris was where I nearly died of the flu.

The boulevard perfume, the nightly coup
of good cheap wine, the loneliness profound:
when I burned hot, Paris was coolly true

because the women there speak French and do
not kiss Americans meaning to astound.
– Paris was where I first imagined you.

We are old now, as Paris is forever new,
as life is you now, as art may still confound:
when we burn deep, every Paris is true.
– Paris is where I am when I'm with you.

Girl on the Bocce Green

The day was slowly dying,
its fiery edges gasifying
the ice-blue sky
into a gorgeous boil of steamy clouds
the dreamy color
of the meat of ripened apricot.

And I was fading, fading
summer slowly on the ossifying
fringe of cocktail-picnic prattle,
glass in hand among the rest,
even while my flickering edges
dwindled down to smoldering regrets –
when at a sudden distance
from the clink of glass and ice,
I spied a young girl sprawled
serenely on the bocce green.

Lolling supine on the lawn,
with long white-jerseyed arms splayed wide
and denim-blue lean legs pegged vertically
like lily stalks with bare-foot blossoms,
she was gazing at the sky it seemed,
seemed to be delving deep
into its dusky fire and ice,
but at the inkling instant when
I might have raised my sights
to share in her perspective,
my emberous eyes were suddenly arrested
by whatever gorgeous force
propelled her rolling cross the green,
rolling log-wise in a swirling fugue
of flashing feet and boiling blondness,

rolling to the bocce chalk-line brink of anarchy
until, undone abruptly on her belly,
she paused, then lingered,
metamorphosed as a momentary sculpture,
her elbows propped upon the grass,
her chin cupped in her hands,
contemplatively peering out to sea,
out to the island on the apricot horizon.

O to be that girl!
to feel the grass, the light, the sky,
to be of them yet not to think of them,
to let time pass yet not to feel its passing.

And as the sculpted moment
of her meditative grace continued,
my eyes followed hers across the sound,
out to the island whose mauve-hued silhouette
was glowing in the gloaming's nimbus,
glowing like a dreamed-of destination,
and so destined I felt myself the boy I was
of burnished evenings on the grass
when I was green and idleness was golden;
I felt the island's shimmer
as a lambent breeze upon my face,
felt free of time's straitjacketing embrace,
felt calm in my elation.

In gratitude I returned my gaze
to tender her my private homage,
to smile my heart at her;
but sitting on the green, then, there were two,
a friend and she, in urgent conversation,
each long and easy in the light,
yet she was somehow changed, transformed,
still beautiful perhaps, but ordinary;

and O, she will forget this,
perhaps already has forgot,
forgot the grass, the light, the sky,
forgot her golden grace,
will not remember what
cannot be borne to memory –
it all must pass away inconsequential.
O to have been that girl!

There

Then, awakening, you see her, there
beside you – naked – sleeping still –
and instantly you realize that nothing
has prepared you for this moment,

nothing you have ever known
explains the selfless curve her hip
carves as it slopes down to her waist,
and in some fine new way *you want her.*

But then you reckon how the pale
side of her arm is cradling her head
and how her sunlit hair cascades
unconsciously across her cheek,

above all how her face seems changed,
oddly hers, but absent *her,*
and you wonder if it is herself
you want or instead this sleeping her –

sleep, that archipelago of island kingdoms,
each governed as a monarchy of dreams,
her dormant face her kingdom's flag,
symbol of her sovereignty,

because in sleep, *you* aren't there for her;
no passport will permit you passage
through the frontier of her dreams,
it is as though you don't exist;

or maybe it's the absence of you
that glorifies your wanting her,
maybe your wanting that confirms
your presence, your very being:

this may seem a paradox
but there is nothing paradoxical
about her naked breasts – no matter
how you contemplate them

their shape and supple heft appear conceived –
ideas deep and elegant in their simplicity –
as with the constants of nature - like Pi,
like gravity, like the speed of light.

Then suddenly her eyes part open,
like butterfly wings
awakening to the warming sun
with hesitant but brilliant color,

and in their wondering gaze,
somehow both innocent and wise,
everything is newly possible,
and you are there – newly there –

and in some fine new way *you love this life.*

Blue Heart

Hailed by name
as I walked up the narrow road that passed his place,
as I looked up from the open book I had in hand,
core struck, heart on edge,
though not quite zero at the bone –
as he, with a salesman's smile, said to me
'You're into poetry, right?'

Were they fighting words, I wondered.
Was flight an option?
Or did I have the right to find my notoriety amusing?
And really, what the hell could he be smiling at?

'You're into poetry, right?'

Why do you ask, I might have parried?
What do you mean, I thought to answer.
'Well yes,' is what I said.

A quarter-century we had been first-name acquainted
though I didn't think I liked the guy –
too glib, too friendly, too damned pleased with life –
'Come here,' he beckoned me onto his patch of lawn –
his *dooryard* Whitman would have termed it,
and so-help-me there were lilacs blooming.

So I joined him on the grass, by a massive boulder there,
eight feet across and high –
'a remnant of the ice age,' he was saying –
boulder, ice age, glacier-in-retreat,
to all of it I nodded my encouragement
as he invited me to circumnavigate the rock,
as he explained how he'd just cleared it
of a generation's brush and vines.

And he went on,
describing how he'd taught his kids to climb the rock,
showing me the hand and foot-holds,
to which I smiled with something like good will –
'But look at this!'
– he stopped us in our glacial tour,
pointing to an indentation in the rock
where long ago a child's hand had painted a blue heart,
the height and size of a childish head.

'I cried when I discovered it,' he said.
His face was open, touchingly sincere,
and then he said, 'You could write a poem about it.'

I might have laughed out loud,
might have shaken my head in proud refusal,
but only a heart of stone could be unmoved by his request –
though in my silent pride
I scoffed at how he thought that poems happen.

Robert Frost called poetry *play for mortal stakes*.
I doubt the stakes Frost had in mind include blue hearts.

And yet something was happening by that rock,
something I did not understand but somehow felt –
he was a man who'd spoken tender thoughts to me,
and I'd been humbled as I heard them.

'We'll see,' I said,
and shrugged the way men do.
If not a promise it was something like consent.

But in the weeks to come I could not do it –
could not make a poem of that damned blue heart.
Though my walks still take me by the rock
I cannot find a poem there –
perhaps it's his to write.

Coincidence on 27

Coincidence is God's way of remaining anonymous... Einstein

1.

Route 27 is the real way
to Mystic – the *Mystical* way, you might say.

They were old and in love:
Joanna and her Seth –
Joey he called her, their private shibboleth
for the cheerful pal she was to him.

With younger friends they'd just
done dinner in a Mystic joint on 27
where they were known and fussed about
like family just arrived for holidays.
By all accounts the group had been convivial –
food good, the wine abundant.
It had been a night well lived.

The world, too, was old that night:
13 billion years of brooding hindsight.

Gaily they departed, Seth and Joey
shuffling steps behind their friends,
walking out into the winter night.
It was early yet, cold and clear,
the crescent moon still rising past the stars,
the tidal river's scent still sharp and briny –
the night was fine, although the light was red,

Warmly wrapped in coats and scarves
they started across the road,
hand-in-hand beyond the painted crosswalk,

following their friends against the light.
Perhaps they didn't see the car,
perhaps they heard it first, looked up,
glimpsing headlights, tires skidding, shrieking,
just before it pounded them upon the pavement.

The Earth, too, was no longer new:
4 billion years and more of hitherto.

Together in the instant on the naked road
Seth reached for her, softly spoke her name, twice,
then forever joined her, dead.
Everybody said that they would always be together.

2.

A mere but fraught 200,000 years
mankind has walked the Earth with hopes and fears.

Carol Belli was alone and old,
a modern mother / divorcée
contentedly retired from teaching school –
like death and taxes, this much was certain.
That fateful evening she had met
a friend in a familiar cozy bar,
that part of Mystic shunned by tourists,
where they had split small bites –
flat breads, fish tacos –
while Carol had a vodka gimlet,
bone cold and limey sharp, the way she liked them.
They talked as women do, smart and funny,
a mutuality of unassertive warmth,
talked of family, of politics.
Carol had another –
she had done her medication,
felt herself the one she liked to be.

When they left, the night was deep and cold,
the moon a white and quiet crescent,
but she was hungry still
and knew McDonald's would be open
at the other end of 27.

    In a world both sacred and profane,
    fate is sometimes this mundane.

The cops efficiently presumed her drunk,
although the test said not –
but through her curbside tears
she allowed as how she wasn't 'sober sober.'
In any case, she hadn't nodded off behind the wheel.
In any case, until too late, she hadn't seen them.
In any case, they were dead.

    And where had God been all that time?
    What was He doing? This cannot be one more mere rhyme.

3.

Then, of course, the law, the lawyers,
then the bargained plea –
to spare an old and ruined woman from the slammer –
then the civil suit and settlement –
one-and-a-quarter mill the price
of loss for Seth and Joey's grieving people,
the most their lawyers said
that shame and policy could pry
from the insurance companies.

Still, Seth and Joey went at once, together,
in their faded but persistent bloom of health,
happy in old age, loved and loving –
really, what better way to go?

except that Carol Belli's life
of ordinary hopes and happiness
was and was not done with.

Well then – can it be both curse and praise
to say God works in mysterious ways?

Winter Moon

Winter. I wake to a bitter night –
hear the wind – recall my love and I are out
of sorts... But the full moon's light

is lovely. What was it we fought about?
Certainly my rage was justified,
but to what end? She was wrong no doubt –

unfair, really – but I'd be mollified
by her apology... The house is still,
her breath the only sound, amplified

by the cold quiet. If I could just distill
this peace, this calm... When did she come to bed?
and why? Asleep she's much more daffodil

than holly – yet what was it she said
enraged me so...? The moonlight fills the room
like breath – her breath. What if I were dead?

Would she grieve or curse or celebrate my doom?
Doom? a bad word for a worse thought...
Her breath – deep – strong – as if she would subsume

my lurching thoughts into the hot
sure engine of her heart, as if its steady thrum
could heal my rage and hurt. Now *there's* a thought!

Why does she love me? Did she come
to bed because of love...? She breathes so well –
each give and take of breath seems to succumb

to, then embrace life's urge, tapping a well

of clear sweet water. Is love like that?
Why do I love *her*? *Who can tell*

may be the answer, with the caveat
that love is not a question. What if I wake
her now to see the moonlight? Then what?

Would she be angry? What if, instead, I wake
her to apologize? Or would that be a new mistake?

Love in Plague Time

The newspaper arrives,
reporting death and disease.
Somewhere a friend is sick.
Throughout the day I feel
the slow steady hum of sadness.

We are an island
surrounded by a sea of virus.
Through the window I watch
you putter in the garden,
squatting on your strong haunches,
hair spraying like straw from under your hat,
hands soiled in the earth.
You stand, survey your work, happy,
then lifting your eyes, meeting mine,
you smile, shyly smile, appearing surprised,
and I want you.

The newspaper rests on the table,
more death and disease.
Somewhere a friend is dying.
Throughout the day I can hear
the nearing echo of grief.

Shedding our tired clothes,
I find your skin tense and ready,
your eyes bright and deep.
The spring light is milky, smooth,
your hands, my hands, are everywhere,
the taste, the aroma, eager and demure.
We are an island of kisses
engulfed by the overwhelming suddenness.

When the newspaper is discarded,
the steady hum of sadness remains.
the nearing echo of grief remains.

The half-moon shines, watery and cool.
We shine, feeling strange and old –
glad for this day, wanting another.
We are an island of humility
in a sea of darkness.
Somehow the moon shines through the window.

On Occasion

For this night's sake let us be an occasion –
let us make a feast of every least
mere moment as though our diligent elation
could raise the dead, as though all our deceased
dear spirits were mingled in the wine,
a rich bouquet of memories – then let
us drink deeply of them. But let's define
our feast of memories by moments yet
to live – above all we should eat and drink
as though this night would never end,
as though for these few fragile hours we think
ourselves immortal, as though on it we could depend.
Do you feel a tender presence in the air?
Our feast is its sacrament, our laughter its prayer.

II. FAMILY MATTERS

I am part of the sun as my eye is part of me. That I am part of the earth my feet know perfectly, and my blood is part of the sea. My soul knows that I am part of the human race, my soul is an organic part of the great human race, as my spirit is part of my nation. In my own very self, I am part of my family.'

D.H. Lawrence

' Zounds! I was never so bethumped with words
Since I first called my brother's father Dad.

Shakespeare

Bethlehem, Again

It's after all about a family,
about one fiercely ordinary man
and his serenely mighty woman, for she
within her bears the un-thought perfect plan.
Together they are traveling the great
and all too common journey home,
even as the world's woes await
the bravely destined child to come.
The dark old story tells itself again,
of prophecies perplexing simple hearts,
of angels terrifying decent men,
and of the parents playing their bit parts.
It after all ends badly – they shall / we shall die.
But listen: can you hear the newborn's urgent cry?

The New Ball

You're a small boy with a fine new ball,
a pumped-up brick-red rubber ball,
on a sunny California morning.

You're with friends at play
in the cracked and cratered asphalt alleyway
between the low apartment blocks.

You're proud of your new ball, which
you bounce among your friends, who
squeal and laugh at the chaotic angles

it makes upon the pitted pavement.
Then Sarah's mother calls for her
out their upstairs kitchen window.

You look up at the window
then at Sarah who you realize is pretty,
but whose eyes have narrowed, darkened,

whose lovely lips have pursed and set –
you see that she's determined to pretend
she doesn't hear her mother's voice.

But the voice starts up again
with an edge you know as anger,
cutting through 'Goddamn it' on the stairs.

The door bursts open and it's Sarah's mother,
her hair a dark helmet,
the lighted cigarette

cornered by magenta lips,
her eyes shining, huge,
and Sarah says 'I didn't hear you,'

as her mother grabs her skinny wrist,
cuffing her head, then again, harder,
saying 'the hell you didn't!'

yanking Sarah through the doorway.
'Mommy no!' The door slams shut,
then up the stairs 'Mommy Mommy!'

the smacking of the belt,
Sarah's wails, again, again –
'Stop it!' you call up to the window,

'Stop!' you cry, but the belt won't stop,
and bellowing a last entreaty
you throw the ball up at the window.

Glass explodes – shivers tinkling,
raining in on sink and floor.
Then sudden silence. The world is still.

You wait, staring at the jagged window frame,
but nothing happens, the world has stopped –
and you bolt, crying, running home

to the apartment, which quiets you –
your father napping for the graveyard shift,
his body curled on one side,

and you sit quiet on the cool wood floor,
frightened, awaiting his awakening.
Then you tell him.

But he doesn't hit you, doesn't yell,
but looks at you in some new way,
his tired eyes searching yours.

'Stay here,' he says, and leaves.
The calm remains. You think
of Sarah's wails, her mother's 'Goddamn it,'

the cigarette, the shattering glass.
You sit still, the stillness strange and new.
When your father comes back, he has a pane of glass,

the first you've ever seen,
strange its thin fragility,
beautiful the way it fills with light,

and you want to touch it, but don't ask to.
Your father takes his tool box, looks at you again.
'I'll be back,' he says, then leaves.

When he returns, the glass is gone
and he doesn't have your ball –
but you decide you shouldn't ask about it.

You wonder – *whose* ball is it now?
You wish he'd tell you something
but don't know what you'd have him say –

only, the breaking glass and silence after
are still there, will not go away –
and you wish you had the ball.

Father and Son

Late at night, in dim exhausted light,
a man lifts boy up from the bed,
gently hoists the boy over his shoulder
like a sack of something essential,
something innocent but heavy,
like flour or rice –
a large boy, sleeping still,
arms dangling down his father's back –
a big boy but my little brother –
the boy asleep so soundly he would wet himself,
Dad lugging him, limp load,
down the hall, to the toilet –
this quiet act of love.

His Hands

My father's hands were beautiful –
grim graceless hooks when hanging slack,
like twin rough stones when clenched,
at work articulate and quick,
their knuckles like ball bearings,
their nails discolored, jagged, sharp
like broken bits of Neolithic tools.
When meeting him a second time
bigger men avoided shaking hands;
when walking with him as a child
I would clasp his index finger.

Sometimes his hands would suddenly
enclose my waifish waist
and sweep me lightly overhead.
Was I breathless then with terror,
or was it pleasure after all?
And in the blue sky of his eyes
I felt myself forever flying,
flying free of anger's gravity
– until he lowered me into his arms,
the cigarette clinched in his teeth,
its burning tip close by my cheek.

Once, crouched small behind the easy chair,
I watched the household tragedy
square off my brother's man-child fists
against my father's fearsome outrage –
man taunting boy to strike first blow,
boy silent but defiantly on guard,
each wronged, each wrong, each broken-hearted
by the instant when my father's sudden fist
met bone-to-bone my brother's cheek –

man self-appalled, boy proudly tearless,
as my mother wailed between them.

And now those hands rest laced
together on his breathless chest,
a sculpted gesture of contented calm
they never knew through long life,
composed expertly for our public grief –
but notice how the crooked fingers
don't altogether *fit* together,
have *not* completely meshed in death
as they couldn't mesh in life;
notice how their twisted tendons
have resisted even this last brittle grace.

Amends

for my Father

Back then, in the ancient Buick
– two-toned red-and-white with white-walled tires –
in that big old Buick beauty of a car
we sat before our house
whose stuccoed modesty belied
the endless overtime you'd worked to buy it,
your mute pure pride in making mortgage every month,
making a California life for us,
and in that Buick moment
you handed me that enigmatic cardboard tube.
I was fifteen.
Nothing like that moment had ever happened.

'What is it?' I asked.
'Open it,' you said.

You wore the suit you'd bought on credit
when they made you salary, an engineer,
having for those many manly years as a machinist
worn a uniform of flannel shirts and khaki pants,
though after dinner you would change to slippers
as you studied for the college courses done at night –
but you looked good then in your fine blue suit,
a handsome silver man, growing old before his time.

From the tube I slid a roll of poster papers
which I flattened on my lap,
taking in an artist's drawings of celestial space,
deep blue-black space and distant stars,
clean, perfect, as space may be,
like comic books, but better, stranger, somehow serious,
and telling of a tall white rocket to the Moon,
topped by a cone-shaped capsule that enclosed
a small, three-legged all-too toy-like landing craft.

Each of the drawings was emblazoned with *Surveyor*
and the name of your employer –
'*Surveyor* is the lander's name,' you said.
'It's the project I've been working on.'
This kind of talk was new and strange to me.

The rocket, as the drawings showed,
would shoot Surveyor at the Moon,
six thousand miles per hour,
its course corrected by Command Center Pasadena,
then as the lander entered lunar gravity,
its own on-board computer
(all the computers I had ever seen were big as Buicks)
would slow Surveyor to a stroll
and gently lower it to rest upon its tripods –
on the Moon!

For the first time in my life
I realized that grown-ups could be crazy,
that my father must be fronting folly.
'This is preposterous,' I said,
with a boy-man's certain confidence.

Another of the drawings showed the phallic shaft-shaped camera
by which Surveyor would photograph the lunar landscape;
another showed a toyish shovel popping from a hatch
and scooping up some lunar soil.
It was all too much.

Through all my youthful television years
the nightly news had shown rockets brightly blowing up
at every stage of launch and flight.
Surveyor seemed self-evidently doomed, absurd, ridiculous –
the very words I used, so proud to use them well.
I was surprised to see them sting you, Dad.
And in that tacit instant I was sorry for your hurt.

But no one in our family apologized, not ever:
I did not yet know how.
In silence you re-rolled the posters;
In silence we went in the house.

One day months later, during school,
Algebra was interrupted by the announcement –
Surveyor had landed.
Miss Poffenberger told us history was being made.
Though confused, astonished by the news,
I told everyone my Dad had worked on it.
At home that night, I awkwardly congratulated you.
You thanked me. That was all.
On television, in speechless wonder
we watched Surveyor's photos of the Moon.
You said nothing, nothing at all.

Dear Father, do you hear me?
I hear only silence.
I hear, as ever, your inability to talk to me,
or was it your unwillingness
to tell your life, your mind, your heart –
or mine to hear.
But if good men deserve good sons
I would be yours, Dad.
I would make amends.

The Bath

All at once – as in a waking dream –
like a pan-sensual movie in my mind –
I feel the warm water – the mild steam –

I see the sink I sat in – the day that shined
into the kitchen window above the sink –
I hear a voice – close – from behind –

my mother's – softly singing – tender link
to the hand pressed firmly on my chest
holding me upright – my skin is pink –

a warm wet cloth has just progressed
across my back – I breathe a faint sweet scent –
I'm naked – a baby – then it ends – the rest

is gone – the wet, the light, the song: all spent –
my mother gone – her voice – its sound – the feel
of comfort, of goodness – what has it meant?

Was it memory or dream? It felt – feels – real –
what's left is luminous calm, deep peace,
and yearning – yearning for more – enough to heal –

enough to make a meaning – to release
in me and all the world this calm, this peace.

Forgiveness

Then you slapped me,
your swift sudden hand knocking me to the floor.
I was a runtish boy of four,
my crime possessing a forbidden toy,
that T.V. cowboy six-shooter,
a chrome-bright tin and plastic pistol
bought and given on the sly by my big brother,
which at night I took from under the bed
to handle, brandish, aim, adore
until the night you found it.
'What's this?' you snarled, teeth bared, eyes
ablaze with a Medusa fury that froze me in its thrall,
and then you slapped me
sprawling, ears ringing, tears and all.
I never saw it coming, Mother.

It was the first of many,
yet so unlike Dad's dismal ritual whippings
when I would stand at terrified attention
for the prologue drawing of the belt,
for the command to fold myself across his knee,
for the slow steady meting out of lashes,
always fewer and not so fierce as I had feared.
When done with it I was surprised
to find myself refreshed and calm.

But *you* stepped into your sudden strokes
with a boxer's focused follow-through,
your anger amping to an athlete's grace of purpose,
but worse and worst your brutal backhand,
wrist whipping the knuckled backside of your hand
to crack against my cheek –
and I, caught always unawares

at the wild instant of your wrath,
never saw your sucker punches coming.
There was no point in crying,
but I cried and ran away,
dismayed at having fallen from your grace.

*   *   *

When newly in New York, I was often asked
why I had left my California –
to which I glibly quipped,
it was as far away as I could get from you, dear Mother.

When you were old you told me on the phone
I was a good man.
Moved, I wanted to return the compliment
but couldn't.

You're dead now, Mom,
leaving me to find forgiveness.
But can we? Can we forgive the dead?
What can it mean, forgiving those
who haven't asked to be forgiven?

I forgive you, Mother –
I don't forgive you.

I forgive you, Mom –
I can't forgive you.

I won't. I will. I have.

Hard Night

for Catharine

It was a hard night, the hardest of nights
as through the long dark hours you worked at birth –
hard the work, hard the pain upon your rites
of first maternity, hard the winter Earth,
and bitter bitter hard the smell of blood,
and so much blood so red upon the sheets.
Like echoes from the hot primeval mud
your groans and growls divulged where life secretes
its bestial mystery: it shone
there in the fierce light of your eyes; it boiled
in your tears; and when the night was done,
it sang out from the child just uncoiled.
Then dawn spread healing on the night's fresh wound,
revealing how a little life may still astound.

Tess Begins

In the strange dark hour
of that not yet morning,
after so hard and much a night,
after your head top's teasing
dalliance at the world's threshold,
you finally slid forth in a fell rush
of blood and slime into my waiting hands,
your head shaped like a thick banana,
your little legs and arms enfolded tightly
like a chicken trussed and ready for the oven.

Though new to birth's immense domain,
though looked at to pronounce your gender,
alas, I saw that you were dead,
in my dismay was dumb to say so,
in any case had never seen such pink
and tender beauty as between your legs.
Then suddenly your eyes popped open
with a blue and searching light,
even as your puckered mouth performed
a perfect O of pure astonished wonder.

Tess is the sound the Earth makes
when in February it dreams of Spring.

New World

What a world lies squirming in my arms!
Smelling of humanity, shaped
just humanly, this worldly new she swarms
with futures fresh escaped.
So *this* is innocence –
this little hand clutched on my finger
with neither good nor common sense
compels an ancient trust. O let it linger!
Yes! and to protect the gentle light
in these undoubting new blueberry eyes
I would believe in God, save money, fight
wars, get a job – anything but cause my own demise:
for, having fathered this new world, I can see
myself become the better man I mean to be.

Needing a Bath

While still the crude umbilical stump clung to her
ruddy belly, I lifted my infant daughter from her cradle,

hoisting her naked up into my arms
and stepped with care into the steaming shower –

her mother was not there, having departed
for a meeting, something important,

leaving me on manly guard –
and in the dense warm fog that billowed

from the shower's spray, I held
my baby to my chest, wet skin to skin,

one hand hefting her curled rump,
the other blanketing her tender rippled back

as to my satisfied surprise,
she settled into silent comfort,

eyes closed, lips puckered –
contentment's infant face.

It was a father's fool experiment, but I
wallowed a long time, wet and warm with her.

Though it may have been meaningless,
I remember it with shining clarity.

Why did I do this?
why disturb the child's serene indifference?

why confound my *own* serenity?
why tempt the fate of her mother's amazed return?

Like most new fathers, I too needed a bath,
but more, much more, I craved a deeper bond.

Needing Sleep

The house was hushed.

You'd just laid the kiddies down to nap
and in our room the light seemed candid,

so I suggested a siesta of our own,
but, not surprisingly, instead of sleep,

I was moved to rest my head upon your belly,
only to find an urgent welcome there,

to feel myself drawn down to where
your green and marshy fragrance gave

way to the tidal taste of coiled fertility –
just when sudden little footsteps came

thumping down the hall toward the door
which you and I forgot to close.

In that instant I flattened over you
and tightly shut my eyes, pretending sleep.

I did not see our toddler daughter enter,
did not see her silently approach,

but felt the sudden closeness of her face,
heard her sniff the strange new scent of us,

breathe us like a dog on foreign turf.
We did not move then as she took us in.

I wondered what was happening in her mind –
the sight and scent of naked parents.

The moment went on for a long time.
When she left and silence filled the house,

I closed the door. Only then did we laugh,
quietly, holding each other,

before drifting into a fine deep sleep.

The Road Home

Then like a vast wet net the drizzly night
dropped down on us. Damn, the road was steep!
Damn, the wind cut deep! And yet despite
the unexpected world, her infant sleep
curled in my sagging arms while your huge heart
thrummed at my side. Far down the bluffs, the sea-
surge boomed and hissed, then silence; and we were part
of it, we were a family.
Father mother child, we were the long road home.
And yes, this much I thought I understood:
you and I were common lovers, had come
the brave way to that night, had felt life's bitter mood;
yet, how was it her tiny trusting face
made of so mean a night a lingering grace?

Step One

for my son

Hope starts small, its frail alloy
conjoining life's bright urge with death's dark worm.
Consider this yearling bit of a boy,

this specimen son, a yowly flesh, a squirm.
Observe now as the pensive stars devise
in him a glory: watch their ancient germ

infect him with a rough resolve to rise
up on his tentative fat feet,
to teeter over the world's yearning eyes.

See how his infant head reels to the beat
of destiny: yes he may fall, should fall,
has always fallen – but the great drums greet

him now as there he stands where he might crawl,
as there he breathes the careful air of thought,
as there the world wobbles in his thrall:

fear flares in his eager eyes, but fraught
upon the pivot point where nature parts
the light from dark, he dreams of balance caught

and held. And here he lifts a foot, here charts
its lurch through time and space, here plants
a first step deep into the future! Music starts!

And now his steps become a dance –
the dance of human possibility,
the dance of choice within a world of chance.

Choose, my boy – choose with humility
to dance the brave ballet of brotherhood,
the gladdening grace-step of civility,

choose the dervy whirl of earth and blood,
the waltz of peace, the circle dance of joy –
O dance, my son, dance the world some good!

Hope starts small – a coy
crude courage. Do not destroy.

Kingdom

That cheap hotel room
just within the massive walls of old St. Malo:
that small, airless, paid-for-in-cash room

whose narrow window overlooked the café terrace,
which that afternoon was slow and murmuring:
that dim hot haven of a room

with yellow walls – or were they yellowing? –
and through whose slightly parted curtains
slanting sunlight glorified a shaft of languid dust:

that moment when I wakened there, my love beside me
napping still, as were our little children head-to-toe
upon the sagging slender bed a step from ours:

that last-room-in-the-inn where, as I lay,
their drowsy give and take of breath dwelled peaceably
amid the distant café clink of cutlery and glassware:

that was my momentary kingdom.

Ballad of Bob and Babs

Babs, my Babs, won't you be true?
Bobbie, o Bobbie, I'll always be for you.

1.

You were in, our folks were out:
for me that's what it was all about.
I was eight, you sixteen,
my evergreen big brother Bob,
and it would mean I'd have
you to myself – or so I thought
'til you said Joel would *make the scene,*
which stung, though Joel was sometimes fun –
but, when together, you and he
felt dangerous, like
when Dad would clean the guns.

I heard Joel's car come from afar,
the ancient rusted Chevy rumbling
its arrival like a throttling tractor.
He came in the back door, like family,
two girls in tow, smelling
hot-house sweet with candy apple lips.
Joel was excited, lit a cigarette –
the kitchen swelled with heat.
One of the girls I recognized as Babs,
her wheat-hued hair, her curved pink sweater.
With a smile you introduced me,
but I could see the girls weren't pleased
at making my acquaintance.
So I left, went into our room,
curled myself into the knee-nook of your desk –
a small dark place I'd thought about –
pulled the chair in, hidden then.

The house grew silent,

a silence bright and sharp with expectation.
Soon stockinged steps came in the room.
I heard the quiet shutting of the door,
heard her moan 'O Bobbie,'
then watched you lie with Babs
upon your bed, and kiss her –
though not like in the movies, hard and clutching,
but softly, gently, lingering,
with a slight conclusive smack –
then a little parting,
her eyes engaging yours with
what seemed wonder, happiness –
then more kissing – different now –
still soft, but longer, urgent,
and there was wrestling on the bed –
I saw her belly, startling, white, your hand there --
then your faces parted, panting, out of breath,
your mouth and cheeks smeared red with lipstick –
and it was funny, O so funny –
I tried but could not stifle it:
my gasped propulsive splutter of a snigger.

You snapped up – looked sharply – saw me there –
I, braced to cry –
Babs, bewildered, propped on elbows –
then you laughed,
your best loud laugh I loved above all others,
clapped your hands, pulled the chair out,
called for Joel, who came, and crouched
to see me, laughed his high-pitched whinny,
and I laughed too, still balled beneath the desk –
but the girls, the girls looked mad.
And there was no more kissing.
When Joel left with the two of them,
you eyed me steadily and said,
'Promise me you won't tell Mom and Dad –'
I never did.

2.

Babs, my Babs, let's seize this day.
No Bobbie, no – we've got to get away.

That bright spring California Sunday morning
the yelling started after breakfast, in
the sunny living room – you versus Mom and Dad.
In the hallway shadows I stood listening:
Mom was crazy outraged – you'd
done something more than ordinarily bad –
and they kept barking *Babs,* her name
in flames of blame, like a fire bomb.
Unusually you took it – no jabs of protest.
Your voice was sullen, without fight,
some kind of shame, some kind of helplessness.
Then we walked to church, we four,
the silence grim,
and no one looked me in the eye.

After church, at home, the silence persisted –
like the L.A. sun's relentless light that slow hot day.
You and Mom had disappeared to other rooms;
Dad stood smoking in the hall, alone,
while in the dining room I sat on the floor,
back against the wall, waiting through the silence.
Then the doorbell rang with its suburban chimes.
'I'll get it,' sang out Dad.
I heard his steps, heard the opening of the door.
'I'm Babs' mother,' said a woman's voice.
'I know,' said Dad –
but oddly he did not invite her in.
The screen door was between them: I could feel it.
And I could feel her standing on the porch,
a long step down from Dad.
And in the moment's stillness, there came
the scent of jasmine and gardenia from the porch.

Then she began to speak, of Babs and you,
spoke your name in nasty blame.
'There's blame enough to go around,' said Dad,
his voice calm, firm –
its quiet force was new to me.
She talked of taking Babs to *Tia-juana;*
when Dad said nothing, she went on,
speaking insistently of money for *Tia-juana,*
her voice becoming a louder hurt,
but shaky, as though she might cry.
Dad's voice cut through:
'I will not pay for anyone to go to *Tia-juana;*
I'll pay to have a wedding at our church.'
She shouted something –
a word I'd never heard before.
'No,' said Dad, like a thumb pressed on a bug.
'We're finished here. Think it over...'
'No, YOU think it over,' she yelped.
'I'm done with this,' he said,
and closed the door. The house was still.
I wondered where Tijuana was
and what would happen there
and whether going there would have stopped the silence.

3.

Babs, my Babs, where did you go?
O Bobbie, forget me, you'll never know.

In that sunny little studio,
with its adorning Chinese shawls and fans,
its gleaming trumpets and the old piano,
where each day you made bebop
in your Venice Beach bohemian shambles,
there you handed me that fateful photo of a girl,

~82~

that sweet-faced, gangly, full-grown girl –
'Who's this?' I asked.
'My daughter, it would seem,' you said –
deliberately provocative in understatement,
but at the look I gave, you added
'You remember Barbara Chadwick?'
'Babs?' I could not help exclaiming,
having not invoked her name since childhood.
You nodded, handing me a letter from
a new dramatis persona, *Danielle,*
postmarked Grand Rapids, Michigan:
my *niece,* it seemed, had found her father.
'What would you do if you were me?' you asked.
Indeed.

What *you* did was become her Dad –
as newly in New York I watched –
as clad in not-quite shining outlaw armor
you became her college wherewithal,
her councilor and means to move out from
her mother's drugs and spongy boyfriends,
for Babs's fate had been to flee
from California's tragic Eden,
to bear your baby
in God-knows-why Grand Rapids Michigan!

But in my self-determined exile
through those New York years,
the story thread I held to was Danielle's,
her own brave choice
to beat the booze and drugs of youth,
to educate herself, launch a career,
above all to become her father's daughter,
as amazed I watched your goodness shine,
your steady words and ready cash,
your pure paternal pride in her.

Despite her bevy of bad boyfriends,
her unplanned pregnancy or two,
you were there for her,
if at too great and difficult a distance.

One Easter she graced California with a visit –
as did I, it happened, nursing heartbreak at the time.
Danielle was dignified and nice,
and fresher, prettier, than I expected –
I found myself both curious and shy about her –
and her little daughter, cute and coltish, with
your black-ish hair, pale skin, your curled lip:
she was your grandchild *it would seem!*
Mom hosted with a ham, plain and dry –
the prolonged, hard divorce from Dad
a sad, still-startling memory,
the wound from which our family never healed.
Among the other family changes, our
demented, if no longer nasty Nana
had come from Pittsburgh, living now with Mom,
the mad and maddening divorcées.
After the long and lively luncheon
came the customary photos posed
upon the jasmine-scented porch
where Dad had long ago confronted Babs's mother –
a scene which I alone had witnessed,
but who would I tell, and why?

You took me by surprise by taking charge
of picture taking – thankless tasks:
to group and pose us, to command our smiles,
to work the camera, yours, a good one –
tasks you'd typically forgo as our
disdainful if reluctant prince.
Yet when you handed me the camera and

proposed a shot of all five generations –
Nana, Mom, and their great
and not-so-great grandchildren,
I grasped a meaning in your motive.
Five generations! I was gob smacked at
the thought of our diffuse, fragmented family
arriving at so un-Californian a photo moment.
Even mad Nana joined the family smile,
which I documented through the camera lens;
seeing that smile, who could have known
how sadly brief it all would be?
Through our years and families to come,
your new career, new daughters to raise up,
new women wooed and then forsaken,
who could have then foreseen the day
you called to say Danielle was sick –
and soon your call to say she was too young to die?
Amid your stoic grief, I wanted you to cry,
wished, perhaps, that I myself could cry.

*　　*　　*

We never spoke of her again, nor of Babs.
The story ended there. Or did it?
I cannot get it out of mind,
the story no one knows but I,
the goddamned sadness of it all.
You too would die too soon,
leaving me to make a meaning of it –
but must every story have a meaning?
Would you, dear brother, want one?
You loved life, sought to do good things.
It came to nothing,
leaving only this and other stories.

III. BISTRO DU NORD

Non, je ne regrette rien,
Ni le bien
Qu'on m'a fait,
Ni le mal –
Tout ca m'est bien egal...

Edith Piaf

(No, I regret nothing.
Not the good
That's happened to me,
Nor the bad –
It's all the same to me...)

Bistro du Nord

(at 93rd Street and Madison Avenue)

Hungry in the solitary way
that seeks a satisfying savor
and perhaps the favor of a quiet corner table,
one that might enable me a new perspective
to divert me from the prospect of another business night
consumed by one more heartless hotel room –
yes, hungry I went in
and meeting with the waiter's Gallic grin
in the New York way of hassled happenstance,
allowed myself to be commanded by his glance
to the restaurant's only empty table.

      At Bistro du Nord
      hunger is the vacuum we abhor.

And there she sat beside me,
at the table on my left so close beside me,
on the sleek banquette we shared along the wall,
so very close that I can still recall the subtle lure of her perfume,
which might have moved me to presume upon her with a compliment,
to comment on her taste in scent,
to introduce myself, to ask her name,
to ask if I might act upon a sudden bent to kiss her pouty lips –
some part or all of which I might have let slip
but for the man who sat across from her:
how could I have neglected to refer to him?
And have I mentioned I was hungry?

      The menu at Bistro du Nord
      bears more than common sustenance, much much more.

She was pretty, of course --

her glossy hair cut short to reinforce
her finely sculpted cheeks, her periwinkle eyes.
How could it have been otherwise
(although in certain of the city's restaurants
a pretty face is no more than a commonplace)?
But O, to have touched *her* face,
to have blindly brailled my fingertips across the landscape of her lips,
to have breached with tender certainty the buttons of her silk chemise
whose billows, styled for chic maternity,
lilted like a sunny breeze through apple trees in blossom,
sweetly musically fragrant . . .
but forgive me: I should mention she was pregnant.

      Ever artfully at Bistro du Nord
      appetite and moderation wage their ancient war.

His tie was elegantly simple,
a silken swatch of rich vermilion,
its expert knot encoded with a perfect dimple,
as was his chin, which framed a thin and earnest mouth:
indeed, he was sincere-appearing
with the sincerity of those who know
they're right and do not hesitate to tell you so.

'I want so much to work this out,'
he said to her, while I, still in some doubt,
pretended to peruse the carte des vins.
But it was then,
just as the waiter stepped before me, poised with pad and pen,
then that we pretended not to hear him add ever so sincerely,
'There's clearly so much more at stake
since you've made up your mind to have our baby.'

      At Bistro du Nord
      we speak of food and wine as seeking a rapport.

'The duck,' I ordered

in a voice that bordered on apology
in the abruptly silent wake of which they bent
on me their furtive glances of astonishment,
as though my sudden being constituted a theology
in which they could not quite believe,
as though a faith were needed to receive
the bread and wine of my discretion.
'Le canard,' confirmed the waiter
with that well-fed smile of his profession,
while they, at loss for what to say,
attended to their soup – a squash purée, I think –
perhaps, I think, grown cold.

      With the Canard du Nord,
        may we recommend an excellent Cahors?

All right, then: must I confess it –
must I admit I wished their drama to continue?
Alas, I too am made of bone and sinew,
and so I sipped my wine
and feigned to read a magazine
reporting on a government grown risible,
even as I tried to will myself invisible
to his refrigerating glance
which chilled me with its swift sidelong reconnaissance,
even as I heard his voice resume
his plaintive case, subsumed to quiet virtue,
saying, 'Every child needs a father,'
urging, 'marriage or, at least, cohabitation,'
while I, in silent consternation
railed *Idiot! Tell her first you love her!*
– though after all I was his sympathizer,
on his behalf longed to apprise her
of the fleeting brevity of life,
the completing levity of love,
longed, in short, to minister a gentle shove,

to say to her, *My dear, that's how life is!*
but just then sensed her hand withdraw from his.

When she spoke,
it was with the quiet razored voice
of one recoiling from a dearth of choice,
as coolly she invoked his wife,
the spitefully litigious Audrey,
cited, too, the tawdry cruelties of their divorce,
and gently touched on Robin,
his precocious bother of a daughter:
did not poor Robin also need a father?
but it was then the timely waiter interrupted,
to inquire discreetly
if their untouched soup were not completely right.
'It's fine,' said he.
Said she, 'I think I've had enough.'

We believe that care in service can restore
even the careworn at Bistro du Nord.

Their impasse was impassioned –
her eyes like stones from staring at perdition,
his necktie perilously near ignition –
yet in that candlelit and glittering world
of silver, glass, and pearly conversation,
in that tinkling realm of unfurled mirth
and damasked-linen civilization,
the surface of their impasse shimmered
with dispassionate decorum,
and it occurred to me:
the restaurant was their chosen forum,
their crucible of strained civility.

As fate would have it
(or was it merely luck?)

she too had duck,
while his fork broached
a pinkly poached filet of salmon,
which suggests that when the spirit starves,
the cause is rarely famine.
Ah but the duck was excellent,
its sauce succinct and savory,
its complement a well-honed remoulade of celeriac,
and O, I might have moaned with pleasure
had I been with her,
might have joined with her in a duet
of hedonistic rhapsodies –
and yet, it seems the salmon failed to please
(or was it that their wine was wrongly white?) –
in any case, with no more than a bite
of fish to nourish his vermilion pride,
he tried once more to talk his way into a bride.

  The food at Bistro du Nord,
  like good table talk, must never bore.

Thus, while she ate duck,
he purported to talk turkey;
as she, in her condition, ate for two,
he, in his rendition, spoke for three.
And yet, however manifold they were,
in doggedness they were a singularity,
he, situating daughter and divorce
conveniently beside the point;
she, demurring, wondering
what was the point;
he, replying that the point
was just as she herself had always stated it;
she, denying ever stating anything
or stating it in quite that way;
he, persisting, bullying,

saying that was how it was;
she, endeavoring to re-define *it,*
pleading, faltering, then steadying herself;
he, maintaining that, whatever it might be,
the situation called for patience;
she, reviving, fortified by fowl,
insisting she would not be rushed to a decision;
he contending it was patience
and decidedly not haste he counseled;
she, retorting she would not be hurried into patience,
not like the long-suffering,
if also too long-suffered, *Uta* –
indeed, another who was not his wife,
indeed, the other other-woman in his life.

        Contentedness at table is a metaphor
        of the enlightened life at Bistro du Nord.

I might have laughed out loud
or might have wept,
except that he,
in whining his denial, vowed
henceforth his strict fidelity.
Imbecile, she must be wooed!
say you want her,
will do anything to have her –
and yet a deeply silent pause ensued
between them: he, perched like a bird
awaiting answer to its song,
and she – absurd! wrong!
that she could be considering his vow!
Yet, even now, I can recall
the palpable sensation of her thought,
can let my hand reach out to touch,
to tenderly caress it –
there can be no suppressing it.

Is it that life seeks for pleasure or
that pleasure welcomes life at Bistro du Nord?

As the moment swelled
within its silent gravity,
I yearned for them to stay,
yearned for them to linger over coffee and dessert
– since I'd partaken of their hurt,
I also wished to share their healing –
but in a gesture whose off-handedness
was less revealing
of improving health
than of a parvenue-ish wealth,
he brusquely summoned forth the bill
– though, coolly and with neither flair nor flash,
it was she who paid, and paid in cash!

If we have pleased, our fondest wish is to encore
your pleasure at Bistro du Nord.

Like a planetary star
serene above the held-breath hush
of an October evening's twilit blush,
she shone above that moment's edge,
waiting, waiting for the waiter to transact
their evening's end, their closing act –
her silken shoulder twenty inches distant
from my haplessly insistent heart.
O what could I say
as she, to my dismay, rose from her seat?
What could I do
as from the table she withdrew?
Even as her scented hand
breezed past my closely guarded gaze,
permitting me to read the polished praise
of candle flame in each nail's perfect manicure,

even then, I said *nothing,*
I did nothing at all.

         *   *   *

I understand it now –
the candles burning low;
the restaurant all but emptied out;
the waiters, bored, assuming me a lout,
pretending to ignore me –
understand it all too well.
It was late, of course –
it's always late –
and, as always, there was music:
the *Little Sparrow* singing bravely of regret,
or rather, of regretting nothing,
her song a French cliché
I cannot now forget.

NOTES

"First Blood" – The setting is Southern California.

"Prayer in Berkeley" – "Telegraph" is Telegraph Avenue.

"Goethe in California" – The setting is Berkeley.

"Ninth Avenue Food Festival" – The setting is New York City.

"Uptown Bus" – The setting is New York City.

"Immortality" – The book she is reading is *Immortality* by Milan Kundera.

"Long Walk with a Good Friend" – The setting is New York City. The "River" is the Hudson.

"Girl on the Bocce Green" – Bocce is a form of lawn bowling. The island is Fisher's Island, which is a part of New York State, though situated off the coast of Connecticut. The setting is Mystic, Connecticut.

"Blue Heart" – The reference "zero at the bone" is from Emily Dickinson. The Walt Whitman references derive from "When Lilacs Last in the Dooryard Bloomed."

"Amends" -- On June 2, 1966, after a 63.5-hour flight, Surveyor became the first American spacecraft to make a soft landing on an extraterrestrial object. During the last three minutes of flight, Surveyor's retro-rockets and thrusters slowed the 649-pound craft from a speed of 6,000 miles per hour to 3 miles per hour, then righted the craft for landing. In doing so, Surveyor conclusively demonstrated the feasibility of landing a manned spacecraft on the moon. Over the next 30 days after landing, Surveyor's camera took 11,000 photographs of the lunar surface, which were telemetrically transmitted to Earth. Surveyor also collected and transmitted data on lunar temperatures and soil content. Jet Propulsion Laboratories designed and executed the Surveyor project. The Missile and Aerospace Division of Hughes Aircraft designed and built the Surveyor landing craft.

"The Road Home" – The setting is Block Island, off the coast of Rhode Island.

"Ballad of Bob and Babs" – in Southern California of the 1950s, it was typical of gringos to mis-pronounce Tijuana as "Tia-juana."

"Bistro du Nord" – Cahors is the "black wine" of Perigord – so-called for its deep purple color. The "little sparrow" is the nickname given by the French to Edith Piaf.

ABOUT THE AUTHOR

Christie Max Williams' debut poetry collection, *The Wages of Love*, won the William Meredith Prize. He is also a writer and actor. Though originally from California and then New York City, he now lives in Mystic, Connecticut, where he and his wife raised their daughter and son. He has worked as an actor and director in California, New York, and Connecticut. He also worked as a fruit vendor in Paris, a salmon fisherman in Alaska, a consultant on Wall Street, a writer for the National Audubon Society, and in leadership posts for non-profit organizations in whose causes he believes. He co-founded and for many years directed The Arts Café Mystic, which is in its 28th year of presenting programs featuring readings by America's best poets, complemented by music of New England's finest musicians. His poetry has been published in journals, magazines, and anthologies, and has won the Grolier Prize, placed second in the Connecticut River Review Contest, and was a finalist for the National Poetry Series and Morton Marr Prize.

This book is set in Garamond Premier Pro, which had its genesis in 1988 when type-designer Robert Slimbach visited the Plantin-Moretus Museum in Antwerp, Belgium, to study its collection of Claude Garamond's metal punches and typefaces. During the fifteen hundreds, Garamond – a Parisian punch-cutter – produced a refined array of book types that combined an unprecedented degree of balance and elegance, for centuries standing as the pinnacle of beauty and practicality in type-founding. Slimbach has created a new interpretation based on Garamond's designs and on compatible italics cut by Robert Granjon, Garamond's contemporary.

Copies of this book can be ordered
from all bookstores including Amazon
and directly from the author,
Christie Max Williams
5 Allyn's Alley
Mystic, CT 06355.
Please send $19 per book
plus $5.00 shipping
by check payable to
Christie Max Williams.

•

For more information on the work of Christie Max Williams,
visit www.antrimhousebooks.com/authors.html.

CPSIA information can be obtained
at www.ICGtesting.com
Printed in the USA
LVHW032203180522
719074LV00004B/673